THE TRANSCENDENT SEED OF ABRAHAM

A PEOPLE FOR YAHVEH

THE TRANSCENDENT SEED OF ABRAHAM

A PEOPLE FOR YAHVEH

BY CHARLES ELLIOTT NEWBOLD, JR.

INGATHERING PRESS

Published by Ingathering Press
P.O. Box 31795
Knoxville, TN 37930-1795
USA

Unless otherwise noted, scripture quotations are taken from the King James Version of the Bible with certain words changed to their modern equivalent; for example, "thee" and "thou" have been changed to "you, " and "saith" has been changed to "says." Some words and punctuation marks have been modernized.

Certain portions of scriptures are italicized to emphasize a point that is made about that scripture.

Readers have my wife, Nancy, to thank for her contributions and edits that made this writing more accurate and reader friendly. Thanks also to those nameless but trusted brothers and sisters in the Lord who reviewed it.

ISBN 0-9647766-4-2
Printed in the United States of America

Outline of text

Introduction
Abram
The Abrahamic covenant
Seven promises to the covenant
Covenant of promise
  based on faith
Formed a people for Yahveh
The land
Sealed in blood sacrifice
An everlasting covenant
Change of nature,
  change of name
Circumcision
Sarai to Sarah
The Son of promise:
- Eliezer
- Ishmael
- Isaac
Abraham tested
Rebekah
Transcendent seed
- Two nations
- Jacob (Israel)
- The birthright
- The blessing of the covenant
- Wrestling with Yahveh
Twelve tribes
Moses and the wilderness
  experience
- The Torah
- More than law
- One continuous story
- Righteous requirement for
  Yahveh's people
Occupying the promised land
The conquest
Period of the Judges
Saul, the first King of Israel
David succeeded Saul
Davidic covenant
Solomon

Divided kingdom: Judah and Israel
Prophets and the promise of a
  New Covenant
Israel/Samaria
Judah
Return from Babylon
Judaism
Maccabees
One crying in the wilderness
Yeshua, the Messiah
The promised seed of Abraham
Implanted by faith
Imperishable (incorruptible) seed
Transcendent land
The will and testament of Yahveh
Yeshua in the Old Covenant
Substitute for the Lamb
A Bride for Messiah
Yeshua fulfilled the
  covenant of Moses
From the outside to the inside
Grace through faith
Yeshua fulfilled the Davidic
  covenant
Kings and priests
True Jews
Satisfied!
Circumcision party
The solidification of Judaism
Early church fathers
Christianity
"Us and Them"
Middles Ages
Modern Judaizers
Falling from grace
The restoration of natural Israel
The End of the Ages
For Yahveh's sake
Conclusion

Note

Preference is given in this writing to the use of God's name, Yahveh, as given to Moses in the wilderness and to the use of Jesus' Hebrew name, Yeshua. No thought is intended to impose this preference upon others.

The Transcendent Seed of Abraham – a people for Yahveh

If only...

If only we knew *whose* we are and *who* we are as sons of God, it would totally, radically change our lives. We have not known entirely *whose* we are and *who* we are, as we ought, primarily because religion[1] has veiled much of it from us. Religion has written our history according to the doctrines and traditions of men and not according to the counsel of the whole word of God.

We have religious groups today who build their faith on Old Covenant laws while others reject the Old and build their faith exclusively on the New Covenant. While many people of different Christian groups believe in the Old and the New Covenants as the Word of God, they fail to see how it is one continuous story. They have difficulty reconciling the God of the Old Covenant with the God of the New even though He is one and the same. The Bible of the Old and New Covenants tell one continuous story of how God—whose name is Yahveh —revealed Himself through a people He chose for Himself. We want to view this story from God's perspective. From the beginning to the end, It is His story about what He intends in all creation. Likewise, it is the story of every true

---

[1] Religion as it is used in this booklet refers to a system of doctrines, creeds, rituals, and patterns of behavior that, when believed and performed, are thought to appease God and merit one's salvation.

believer in Yeshua (Jesus) the Messiah. This is your story from beginning to end.

The story of mankind began in a garden called Eden with a man and woman. However, for the purpose of this writing, let us begin a little later in time as told in Genesis chapter 12 with a man named Abram—later named Abraham.

Abram

It was an ordinary day in the life of Abram, around the year 2060 B.C. He and his wife Sarai lived with his father Terah in Haran. The humdrum of his day was suddenly interrupted by a voice from an unseen presence. He could not ignore the voice. Though he likely had never heard it before, he knew intuitively that it was the voice of the Creator of the heavens and the earth.

Abram's life was changed forever by that encounter with the Creator. Moreover, the course of history was set for all time to come. Nothing could alter it though many have tried. We begin our story with him.

The Abrahamic covenant

Yahveh, the Creator, commanded Abram saying, "Get out of your country, and from your kindred, and from your father's house, unto a land that I will show you. I will make of you a great nation, and I will bless you, and make your name great; and you shall be a blessing. And I will bless those who bless you, and curse him who curses you: and in you shall all families of the earth be blessed." Gen. 12:1-3. Thereby, with these words, Yahveh entered into covenant with him.

Our story is illustrated with a timeless-line, diagrammed below, beginning with Abram and extending to eternity. This covenant with Abram is everlasting, eternal; therefore, this timeless line is necessarily everlasting, eternal. It illustrates Yahveh's eternal purposes. Significant names and events will be added above the line to show movement in our story throughout history.

$$\longrightarrow$$

The timeless line

Seven promises to the covenant

This covenant with Abram has seven unconditional promises. The responsibility to carry out the terms of this covenant are upon Yahveh Himself and not upon Abram. Yahveh initiated the covenant. This is what He wants for Himself and He will have what He wants. What He commands will come about. He is faithful.

First, Yahveh told Abram that He would *show* him a land, a land that He later gave to him. The land is an essential part of the covenant. The people to whom it belongs, belongs to it. They are associated one with the other. It has prophetic implications even today.

Then, Yahveh promised Abram that He would make of him a great nation. This is linked to a later promise to give Abram an heir. Yahveh promised Abram that his seed[3] would be as the dust of the earth: so that if a man can number the dust of the earth, then shall His seed also be numbered. Gen. 13:16. He later told Abram that his seed would be as numerous as the stars of heaven. Gen. 15:5.

Yahveh promised Abram that He would bless him. The scriptures later claim that Abram was so blessed with earthly possessions that the land would not sustain both him and his nephew Lot, so they separated themselves.

Yahveh promised Abram that He would make his name great. Even to this day, is there anyone who has not heard of the name

---

[3] The term *seed* has multiple applications throughout this text. It has to do with human sperm, particularly that of Abraham and his descendants after him. It has to do with descendants, and later in this text it is associated with the Word of God and the Son of God. (I often use the term seed to include all of these meanings.)

3

Abraham? He is the father of millions of Jews who are descendants of Isaac and millions more of Arabs who are descendants of Ishmael. The case can be made that three religions claim Abraham as their father: Judaism, Christianity, and Islam.

Yahveh promised Abram that He would make him a blessing to others. In fact, He declared that in Abram all the families of the earth would be blessed. The word for family used here also means clans, tribes, and peoples. It is plural.

Yahveh promised Abram that whoever blessed him He would bless.

Yahveh promised the reverse as well—that whoever cursed Abram, He would curse. We cannot curse Abraham or the seed of promise and expect to be blessed of Yahveh.

Various aspects of this covenant were repeated and confirmed at subsequent times in Abram's life.

Covenant of promise based on faith

Yahveh told Abram to get out and go to a land that He would show him. According to Hebrews 11:8, Abram had no idea where he would be going; nevertheless, he obeyed. He acted on pure and simple faith.

Abram believed Yahveh, and his faith was accounted to him for righteousness. Gen. 15:6. Abram was not accounted righteous because of any works or religious deeds he performed because righteousness cannot be earned. It cannot be worked up. Yahveh alone is righteous. Therefore, righteousness had to be accredited (ascribed, imputed) to him. Yahveh ascribed righteousness to Abram because Abram believed. His obedience was the proof of his faith.

"Abram was seventy-five years old when he went out from Haran. He took Sarai his wife, and Lot his brother's son, all their substance that they had gathered, and the persons that they had

4

gained in Haran; and went forth to go to the land of Canaan." Gen. 12:4,5.

Yahveh made a promise to Abram and he believed; thus, making *this a covenant of promise based on faith (faithfulness)*, diagrammed on the timeless line below.

Covenant of promise based on faith
——————————————————————————————————→

Formed a people for Yahveh

In making this covenant with Abram, Yahveh began to form a people for Himself. They were to be a people of His own making to fulfill His own purposes. Yahveh spoke through Moses in the wilderness saying, "If you will obey My voice indeed, and keep My covenant, then you shall be a peculiar treasure unto Me above all people: for all the earth is Mine. And you shall be unto Me a kingdom of priests, and a holy nation." Exod. 19:5,6. This promise of destiny is repeated in Deuteronomy 7:1-11 and 26:16-19.

The land

Abram and his seed were promised a particular piece of real estate. First, He told Abram "to go to the land that I *show* you." Then He said in Genesis 12:7, "Unto your seed will I *give* this land." Genesis 13:15 declares that it *was given* forever. Nowhere in scripture has Yahveh deeded that piece of real estate to another. It does not matter who else claims ownership or tries to occupy it; they do not own it. It belongs perpetually and forever to Abram and his seed and his seed belong to it.

The tombs of Israel's patriarchs have been enshrined in the land of Israel and memorialized for millenniums as permanent markers certifying that the land has always been theirs. Add to that the multitude of sacred Jewish and Christian shrines throughout the land that documents the historicity of Israel's possession.

5

Yahveh told Abram to walk through the land in the length of it and in the breadth of it, for He would give it to him. Gen. 13:17. If you have any doubt who owns the land once called Palestine, now called Israel, then read the deed—the first five books of the Old Covenant.

The land was Yahveh's to give. The prophet Joel, speaking the heart of Yahveh, said, "I will also gather all nations, and will bring them down into the valley of Jehoshaphat, and will plead with them there for My people and for My heritage Israel, whom they have scattered among the nations, and parted *My land*." Joel 3:2.

Sealed in blood sacrifice

The covenant Yahveh made with Abram was sealed in a blood sacrifice. Yahveh assured him, "Fear not, Abram: I am your shield, and exceeding great reward." Abram pled with Yahveh, "What will you give me, seeing I go childless?" Yahveh told him that one would come forth out of his own bowels that would be his heir and his heirs would be as numerous as the stars in the heaven. Gen. 15:1-5.

Yahveh then reassured faithful Abram that He was the one who had brought him out of Ur of the Chaldees to give this land as an inheritance. Abram asked, "Whereby shall I know that I shall inherit it?" Gen. 15:7-8.

Yahveh answered Abram. "Take Me a heifer of three years old, and a she goat of three years old, and a ram of three years old, and a turtledove, and a young pigeon." Abram took these to himself and divided them in his midst and laid each piece one against another, but he did not divide the birds. When the fowls (vultures) came down upon the carcasses, Abram drove them away. Gen. 15:9-11.

What then is the connection between these animal sacrifices and Yahveh's promise of an heir to Abram? In cutting this blood sacrifice with Abram, Yahveh pictured how He planned to deliver upon His promise of an heir.

An heir is one who inherits something. For there to be an inheritance, the one who has something to leave to an heir must die. This means someone would have to die in order for Abram and his seed after him to gain Yahveh's promised inheritance. This was not the appointed time for that to happen. So Yahveh initiated animal sacrifices to picture for us the promise of a Messiah who would in time die for us, making us heirs and joint-heirs of the promised inheritance. We will come to this later on in our timeless line.

The vultures of the air that came down to devour the carcasses are a type of demonic powers working under the authority of Satan. His scheme throughout history is to try to steal the covenant with its promises from Yahveh's elect. Anything that produces disbelief and disobedience is obviously not of faith, but is intended to steal the inheritance that was promised to the heirs of Abram. If Satan cannot steal the inheritance, he will try to kill the heirs—anything to destroy the seed.

An everlasting covenant

The enemy's attempt to destroy the seed will be to no avail, because the covenant is everlasting. Yahveh confirmed His promise to Abraham saying, "I will establish My covenant between Me and you and your seed after you in their generations for an *everlasting covenant*, to be a God unto you, and to your seed after you. I will give unto you, and to your seed after you, the land wherein you are a stranger, all the land of Canaan, for an *everlasting possession*; and I will be their God." Gen. 17:7-8.

The word for everlasting in Hebrew has been translated ever, old, perpetual, evermore. This covenant is not time-bound or earth-bound. It exists in the eternal, spiritual realm of the kingdom of Yahveh. That realm is non-dimensional and is not subject to time, space, and distance. It does not have length, depth, and height as we understand those dimensions. Whatever was, is.

7

Whatever is, will be. Whatever will be has always been. All things in Yahveh are present tense. He is the great I AM which is the meaning of His name, Yahveh—the beginning and the end, the alpha and the omega.

The promise of the covenant with Abram has no end. What Yahveh said would happen will happen because it is already a reality in the realm of His kingdom. This is a mystery to us and hard to understand, but nonetheless real.

Change of nature, change of name

Abram was 99 years old when Yahveh appeared to him again and said, "I am the Almighty God; walk before me, and be perfect. And I will make My covenant between Me and you, and will multiply you exceedingly." Abram fell on his face and Yahveh talked with him saying, "As for Me, behold, My covenant is with you, and you shall be a father of many nations. Neither shall your name any more be called Abram, but your name shall be Abraham; for a father of many nations have I made you." Gen. 17:1-5.

Abram means "exalted father." Abraham means "father of a multitude." His name is prophetic in that it perpetually proclaims Yahveh's promise that was given in the covenant. He was now destined to be the father of a multitude of peoples who would form the covenant people of Yahveh.

The words of the covenant to Abram were not just words that existed outside of Abram that he heard with his natural ears, words that he had to try to live up to. These were words of life to Abram because they were words from Yahveh who is Life. These were words that came into him and pierced his soul and spirit. These words made it impossible for him to disbelieve because they became a part of who he was. Thus, through faith, he was accounted righteous by Yahveh. Before faith came, he was not righteous;

8

afterwards, he was. Whereas before he was of his natural father, Terah, from the land of Ur; now he was of his heavenly father, Yahveh. These words of life changed Abram's life. Moreover, he had a change of nature.

Circumcision

Once again Yahveh confirmed His covenant with Abraham, then, concerning the covenant, asked him to be obedient in one thing only. He said, "This is My covenant which you shall keep between Me and you and your seed after you. Every male child among you shall be circumcised. And you shall circumcise the flesh of your foreskin; and it shall be a token of the covenant between Me and you. And he that is eight days old shall be circumcised among you, every male child in your generations...he that is born in your house, and he that is bought with your money must be circumcised: and My covenant shall be in your flesh for an everlasting covenant." Gen. 17:10-13.

Follow the sequence here. First, Yahveh entered into covenant with Abram. That was a "done deal." Nothing could change what He had set in motion. When the Word came to Abraham, it changed his nature and he could not do other than believe in it. He could not do any other but to follow this God that had changed his nature and changed his name. His faith was attributed as righteousness. Nevertheless, Yahveh asked Abraham to obey Him in this strange new requirement. Why? Because circumcision was simply a token, or a sign of the covenant Yahveh had made with Abraham and not the means whereby Abram was made righteous. It was the outward sign to the world foreshadowing the circumcision of our hearts. Many people wear wedding rings, but the ring does not make the marriage. It is merely a sign or token of the marriage. So it was with circumcision. That is to say, circumcision did not determine Abraham's righteousness. Righteousness was accredited to

9

him because of his faith in Yahveh and in Yahveh's promises.

We add Abraham to the diagram below.

Abraham

Covenant of promise based on faith
→

Sarai to Sarah

As it was with Abraham, so it was with Sarai. In order for her to be the mother of this covenant people, she too had a change of nature, and with this change of nature came a change of name.

Yahveh said to Abraham, "As for Sarai your wife, you shall not call her name Sarai, but Sarah shall be her name. And I will bless her and also give you a son by her; then I will bless her, and she shall be a mother of nations; kings of peoples shall be from her." Gen. 17:15-16. According to Strong's concordance, Sarai means "princess" and Sarah means "noble woman." Young's concordance suggests that Sarai means "Yah is prince" and Sarah means "princess." Unger's Bible Dictionary says Sarai might have meant "contention."

Sarah was chosen. Abraham and Sarah, as were their heirs who followed them, were in the mind of Yahveh before the foundation of the earth. It was not accidental that Sarah became the covenant wife of Abraham. She, too, was known and appointed by Yahveh before the foundation of the world. It could not have been any other woman. It had to be Sarah. And so it was.

The Son of promise

Eliezer

The covenant had been made with Abraham and his seed after him. Abraham was getting old and Yahveh had not yet given him a descendent from his own flesh. Before Abram's name was changed, he asked Yahveh what he would give him since he was childless. He bargained with Yahveh to accept Eliezer of Damascus, who had been born in his house, to be his heir. Yahveh answered him, "This man will not be your heir; but one who will come forth from your own body shall be your heir." Gen. 15:1-4.

Ishmael

Still, no heir was born to Abram from his own body. Abram's wife, Sarai, before her name was changed, had not birthed him any children. After they had lived ten years in the land of Canaan. Sarah, not believing she would have a child, gave Hagar, her Egyptian maid, to Abram as his wife, and Ishmael was born. Gen. 16:1-3. Ishmael means, "El (God) will hear."

Contention arose between Sarai and Hagar, and Hagar was driven out of Sarai's presence into the wilderness. The angel of Yahveh spoke to her there by a spring of water and told her to return to Sarai and submit to her authority as her maid. Regarding Ishmael, the angel of Yahveh promised her that He would greatly multiply her descendants so that they, likewise, would be too many to count. One covenant was made with Abraham while the other was made with Hagar. The first was made with the patriarch of a people. The latter was made with the matriarch of a people.

As for Ishmael, the angel of Yahveh prophesied that "he will be a wild donkey of a man. His hand will be against everyone and everyone's hand will be against him. He will live to the east of all of his brothers." The Arab's are the descendants of Ishmael.

Isaac

Because of this covenant with its promises, Sarah was destined to give birth to a son whose name would be Isaac. Yahveh affirmed, "I will establish My covenant with him for an everlasting covenant, and with his descendants after him." Gen. 17:19-20. Isaac was the son of promise.

Abraham was ninety-nine years old when Yahveh renewed his promise to him and told him that Sarah would bear him a son. Abraham fell on his face with laughter because Sarah was old and beyond her natural ability to bear children. But a miracle was on the way! Yahveh said that Sarah his wife would bear him a son and he was to call his name Isaac. When Sarah heard of it, she too laughed at the thought of it. Gen. 18:9-11 and 21:6. Isaac means, "he laughs."

We add Isaac to the diagram below.

Abraham
Isaac

Covenant of promise based on faith

→

Abraham tested

Yahveh, who often made use of allegory throughout His written word and who knows the end from the beginning, predetermined that Abraham would picture Yahveh as Father, and Isaac would picture the Son of Yahveh as the sacrificial Lamb.

So Abraham was tested. Yahveh called out to Abraham and told him to take Isaac (his only son born of his covenant wife Sarah) and offer him for a burnt offering upon a mountain in the land of Moriah. Abraham took wood, fire, and his son and went where he was told. Isaac did not know what Yahveh had told his father, but he noticed that something was missing. "My father," he asked, "look, the fire and the wood, but where is the lamb for a burnt offering?" Abraham assured him that Yahveh would provide for Himself a lamb for the burnt offering. Abraham took the knife to slay his son, and the angel of Yahveh called out of heaven to him and told him not to lay his hand upon the lad. "For now I know that you fear God, seeing you have not withheld your son, your only son from Me." Abraham saw a ram caught in a thicket by his horns. He went and took the ram and offered it up for a burnt offering instead of his son. Gen. 22:1-14.

Rebekah

Not only is Isaac pictured as the sacrificial son, the Lamb of Yahveh, he is also pictured as a type of Messiah who takes a bride unto Himself. Abraham sent his servant to the land of his kinsmen to find a wife for Isaac. Isaac was not to take a wife from among the Canaanites.

Isaac's bride-to-be was chosen beforehand by Yahveh and was confirmed by Abraham's servant. When Rebekah consented to return with the servant to his master, her family blessed her saying, "You are our sister, you will be the mother of thousands of millions, and let your seed possess the gate of those who hate them." Gen. 24:58-60. This blessing is similar to the promise Yahveh gave to Abraham saying, "That in blessing I will bless you, and in multiplying I will multiply your seed as the stars of the heaven, and as the sand which is upon the sea shore; and your seed shall possess the gate of his enemies." Gen. 22:17.

Transcendent Seed

Wait just a minute though! We have a problem. Did not Yahveh say to Abram, "...to you and to your seed after you?" Was not Ishmael Abram's seed? Did not Abraham have other sons born to him by concubines after Sarah's death? Were they not all circumcised? Yet, the covenant passed only to Isaac. How do we account for this discrepancy?

Consider that there are two different natures of seed at issue here. Abraham's biological sperm was the same for all. But there is more than biological sperm involved here. Yahveh introduced a

13

whole different kind of seed/offspring. This seed was to a degree biological, but it was more than biological. This seed was chosen beforehand in the foreknowledge of Yahveh. It was impregnated with the eternal, living word of Yahveh in the form of a covenant with promises. Therefore, it transcends (goes above and beyond the limits of) earthly, natural, biological seed. To coin the phrase, *it was transcendent seed.* Though having to do with sperm, this seed refers to a particular, peculiar, chosen, and transcendent people of promise based on faith—a people of Yahveh's own choosing.

The transcendent seed implants the Life of Yahveh in His chosen ones when it is received by faith. By faith Abraham believed and righteousness was credited to him. One can be called and chosen as a descendent of Abraham, yet not be faithful. The election is to no avail if it is not mixed with faith.

This peculiar seed and this timeless line, though they are experienced in history, are eternal and pertain to the kingdom of Yahveh. Though they touch earth, they transcend the earthly realm. Though they permeate the natural realm, they transcend the natural realm and are supernatural in essence. They picture in the natural Yahveh's eternal purposes and plans in the spiritual realm of His kingdom—a kingdom that is not of this world.

This covenant was a covenant of promise based on faith. It defies all logic and reason. Faith is the distinguishing mark of this transcendent seed. "For the promise, that he should be the heir of the world, was not to Abraham, or to his seed, through the law, but through the righteousness of faith." Rom. 4:13.

THE OBJECTIVE OF THIS STUDY IS TO FOLLOW THIS TRANSCENDENT SEED OF ABRAHAM THROUGH THE AGES AS ILLUSTRATED IN THE TIMELESS LINE THAT WE MIGHT KNOW *WHOSE* WE ARE AND, IN THE PROCESS, COME TO KNOW *WHO* WE ARE.

Two nations

Jacob (Israel)

The promise was made to Abraham, passed on to his seed Isaac and onward to Isaac's seed, Jacob, but not without struggle.

Rebekah was barren until Yahveh heard Isaac's plea and she conceived. She was pregnant with twins who struggled against each other before they were born. She asked Yahveh why she was this way and He answered, "Two nations are in your womb, two peoples shall be separated from your body; One people shall be stronger than the other, and the older shall serve the younger."

The first twin son was born. He came out red and hairy, so they called him Esau which literally means, "hairy." Afterwards his brother came out holding on to Esau's heel. They called him Jacob which literally means "one who takes the heel." It means "supplanter" and "deceiver."

The birthright

By right of birth, Esau was due the blessing of the firstborn, but he despised his birthright and sold it to Jacob for a bowl of stew. Gen. 25:29-34. Later, on the prompting of his mother, Jacob tricked his father into pronouncing the blessing of the firstborn over himself; thus, stripping it from Esau. Gen. 27. So Esau had neither the birthright nor the blessing that accompanied it.

Isaac blessed Jacob saying, "Therefore may God [Yahveh] give you of the dew of heaven, of the fatness of the earth, and plenty of grain and wine. Let people [nations] serve you, and nations bow down to you. Be master over your brethren, and let your mother's sons bow down to you. Cursed be everyone who curses you, and blessed be those who bless you." Gen. 27:28-29. Note again the similarities between this and the covenant made with Abraham.

Esau was enraged at Jacob's deception and the loss of his blessing and threatened to kill Jacob. Esau lifted up his voice and wept, pleading with his father: "Have you only one blessing, my father? Bless me also, O my father!" Gen. 27:38.

Isaac answered with a mixed message: "Behold, your dwelling shall be of the fatness of the earth, and of the dew of heaven from above. By your sword you shall live. You shall serve your brother; and it shall come to pass, when you become restless, that you shall break his yoke from your neck." Gen. 27:39-40.

Esau was given temporal prosperity, but in the context of adversity. He took wives from the women of Canaan. Esau became the nation, or tribe, of Edom which literally means, "red." Gen. 36:8. He was the father of the Edomites who later prohibited Moses and the Israelites from passing through their land in Mt. Seir. Num. 20:14-21.

The blessing of the covenant

More was at stake for Esau than losing his birthright and blessing. The Abrahamic covenant by all natural rights should have passed to him, but was passed to Jacob instead. Yahveh knew and chose Jacob before the world was. These events had to take place at set times in the drama of Yahveh's intervention upon human history.

Isaac told Jacob to return to the house of Rebekah's brother in Padanaram to take a wife for himself. Before leaving, Isaac pronounced the Abrahamic covenant upon him. He said, May "God Almighty bless you and make you fruitful and multiply you that you may be an assembly of peoples. And give the blessing of Abraham to you and your descendants with you that you may inherit the land in which you are a stranger that God [Yahveh] gave to Abraham." Gen. 28:3-4.

On his way to Padanaram, Jacob dreamed of a ladder extending from earth to heaven with angels ascending and descending on it. Yahveh stood at the top of it and confirmed the Abrahamic covenant saying, "I am Yahveh God of Abraham your father, and the God of Isaac. The land whereon you lay, to you will I give it and to your seed. Your seed shall be as the dust of the earth, and you shall spread abroad to the west, and to the east, and to the north, and to the south. In you and in your seed shall all the families of the earth be blessed. And, behold, I am with you, and will keep you in all places where you go, and will bring you again into this land; for I will not leave you, until I have done that of which I have spoken to you." Gen. 28:13-15. Jacob called the place Bethel, meaning "house of God."

Once again we see the transcendent seed of the covenant passing to one of Abraham's descendants and not another.

Wrestling with Yahveh

Jacob went to Padanaram and met his maternal uncle, Laban. Laban tricked Jacob into marriage with Leah, his firstborn daughter, before he allowed him to have Rachel whom Jacob loved. Jacob served Laban another seven years for Rachel. Altogether, he worked for Laban twenty years before fleeing from him. Gen. 31:38. During those years, Jacob prospered. Gen. 29.

Jacob left Padanaram and sent messengers ahead of him with peace offerings for his brother Esau. He stayed the night by the ford of Jabbok. A Man, confirmed by the scriptures to be Yahveh, wrestled with Jacob all night. The Man did not prevail against Jacob, so He touched the socket of his hip causing him to limp. The Man said to Jacob, "Let me go, because day breaks." Relentless as Jacob was to receive the blessing of Yahveh, he refused to let go demanding, "I will not let you go, except you bless me."

The Man asked, "What is your name?" "My name is Jacob," he answered. Did Yahveh not know Jacob's name? Of course He did. He asked him his name in order to set him up for what was to come.

The Man declared, "Your name shall no more be called Jacob, but Israel. For as a prince you have *power* with God and with men, and have prevailed." Gen. 32:28. The word *power* in Hebrew means contend, have power, persist, exert oneself, or persevere. In other places this word has been translated "prince;" meaning, to be or act as prince, rule, contend, have power, prevail over. The King James Version included this meaning in this passage, adding the phrase, "for as a prince." Other translations have omitted the reference to prince.

That night Jacob, just as had happened to his grandfather Abraham, experienced a change of nature and with it came a change of name. That he prevailed against Yahveh can be understood only in this light. No longer was he merely a son of man in the flesh, but had become a son of Yahveh in the spirit by virtue of the covenant. As it was with Abraham, so it was with Jacob. The word of the covenant not only came to him but also came *into* him and changed his nature. After that and because of that, he was considered a prince and had power with God and with men. If Yahveh is the King, then all of His sons (and daughters) are princes. If princes, then we have power with God and with men. If only we knew!

Jacob asked the Man His name but was not given it. Nevertheless, the Man blessed him there. Jacob called the place Peniel saying, "I have seen God face to face and my life is preserved." Gen. 32:30.

After Jacob came out of Padanaram, Yahveh once again confirmed both Jacob's name change and the promise of the covenant. At that time, Yahveh declared that He was El Shaddai: God Almighty. He commanded the blessing upon Jacob saying, "Be fruitful and multiply; a nation and a company of nations shall be of you, and kings shall come out of your loins. The land which I gave Abraham and Isaac, to you I will give it, and to your seed after you will I give the land." Gen. 35:11-12.

We add Jacob to the diagram below.

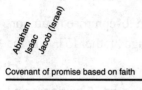

Covenant of promise based on faith

Twelve tribes

Jacob had twelve sons born to him. Rueben, Simeon, Levi, Issachar, Judah, and Zebulun were born to Leah. Joseph and Benjamin were born to Rachel. Dan and Naphtali were born to Bilhal, Rachel's maidservant. Gad and Asher were born to Zilpah, Leah's maidservant. Gen. 35:22b-26.

The transcendent, covenant seed began with Abraham, passed to Isaac not Ishmael, and then to Jacob not Esau. From there the seed passed to the twelve sons of Israel, but a peculiar lineage is traced through Judah of which we will later take special note.

We add the twelve tribes of Israel to the diagram below.

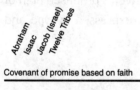

Covenant of promise based on faith

Moses and the wilderness experience

When Yahveh sealed His vow to Abram with the blood sacrifice (Genesis 15), Abram fell into a deep sleep and a horror of great darkness fell upon him. Yahveh said to Abram, "Know of a surety that your seed shall be a stranger in a land that is not theirs, and shall serve them; and they shall afflict them four hundred years.

Also I will judge that nation whom they shall serve and afterward they shall come out with great substance." Gen. 15:13-14.

This word was fulfilled after Jacob's son Joseph rose to authority in Egypt. He brought his family and his aged father to live in the land with him there.

Their descendants became slaves to the Egyptians and remained in bondage for four hundred years. In the appointed time around 1520 B.C., Yahveh heard the cry of His people, Israel, and raised up Moses to deliver them out of bondage. After miraculously crossing the Red Sea, they went into the wilderness where they wandered for forty years. The first generation of Israelites who came out of Egypt was not able to enter into the Promised Land because of unbelief.

Yahveh tested them in the wilderness. They experienced many miseries—due mainly to their stubbornness, rebellion, disbelief, and idolatry—yet, many good things also happened. Yahveh sustained them miraculously on daily manna. He gave them the Torah (law), the tabernacle, and the celebration of worship through His appointed feasts. Though they had no idea what these things represented, they were given as symbols of Yahveh's promised plan of redemption in the Messiah to come. They expressed in type and shadow Yahveh's eternal plan in history.

We add Moses to the diagram below.

Abraham Isaac Jacob (Israel) Twelve Tribes Moses

Covenant of promise based on faith ⟶

The Torah

While in the wilderness at Horeb, Moses went up and down Mount Sinai to bring back a word from Yahveh. The people gathered around the foot of that mountain on one occasion to see Yahveh. Thunder, lightning, and a thick cloud covered the mountain. The sound of a trumpet was very loud and they all trembled. Yahveh spoke to Moses by voice. Ex. 19.

It was on that mountain that Yahveh gave them the Ten Commandments. Ex. 20:1-17. He gave many other laws, statutes, and ordinances that are called the Torah.

More than law

What is meant by the Torah? Torah has been translated Law, specifically as it was given to Moses by Yahveh in Horeb, but it embraces more than the Ten Commandments. In Exodus 24:12, Yahveh instructed Moses to go up to Him in the mountain and He would give him three things: "tables of stone, and a law [torah], and commandments which I have written; that you may teach them." The Torah was the inheritance of the congregation of Jacob. Deut. 33:4.

By the time of Joshua, the Torah was referred to as a book. Jos. 1:8. Joshua built an altar to Yahveh, the God of Israel in Mount Ebal, gathered the people, and "read all the words of the Torah, the blessings and cursings, according to all that is written in the book of the Torah." Jos. 8:34. More than the Ten Commandments are included here.

Torah, however, does not mean "law" as that term is understood in Western languages. It is not about posting a list of rules that are laid down for us to do so we might be right with Yahveh. It includes laws and regulations, but is much more than that. It includes all that is in the first five books of the Old Covenant.

21

The Torah conveys Yahveh's passionate revelation of Himself, of His creation and His created ones, of His calling forth and setting apart a people for Himself, of His righteous requirements for their worship and behavior, and of His provision for their salvation.

Moreover, the Torah is the recorded saga of Yahveh's word as it is dynamically and vividly expressed through His people, Israel. We cannot separate the Torah from Yahveh. The one defines the other. We would not know Yahveh were it not for the Torah, and there would be no Torah were it not for Yahveh. The one reveals the other.

One continuous story

The Torah is one continuous story that tells how Yahveh created a people, then called a people out of this created people to be a people unto Himself.

These five books of the Torah can be reasonably divided into seven time periods:

- How Yahveh dealt with mankind from creation to Abraham. Gen. 1-11.

- How Yahveh set apart a covenant people for Himself through Abraham, Isaac, and Jacob. Gen. 12-36.

- How Yahveh tried this people in the furnace of affliction in Egypt through Joseph and his brothers. Gen. 37-50.

- How Yahveh led this people from Egypt into the wilderness to prepare them for the Promised land. Ex. 1-18.

- How Yahveh entered into covenant with this people through Moses in Sinai, setting forth His righteous requirement for them. Ex. 19-Num. 10:10.

- How this people wandered in the wilderness in rebellion against Yahveh. Num. 10:11-36:13.

- It closes with Moses's farewell address which retells the story in the wilderness. Deut. 1-34.

The Torah, as a volume of work, ends in the wilderness. It is fundamental to all else that unfolds in the Old and New Covenants, but it is far from the end of the story or of Yahveh's revelation of Himself. The rest of the story was (and is) yet to be told.

We add another line on our diagram to illustrate how the Torah fits in with the covenant Yahveh made with Abraham.

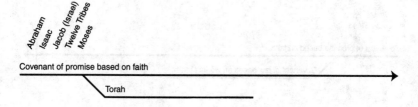

Righteous requirement for Yahveh's people

Exodus 24:7 tells us that all the words Moses wrote were referred to as *the book* of the covenant. If the Torah is the book of the covenant and the covenant consists of the first five books of the Old Covenant, then both the covenants with Abraham and Moses are included in it. This raises interesting questions: Are these two separate covenants? Did the Mosaic covenant replace the Abrahamic covenant? Essentially, these two covenants are two parts of one. *The covenant made with Abraham formed a people for Yahveh. The covenant made with Moses set forth the righteous requirement of this people.* The latter did not replace the former.

Yahveh knew the people would not be able to keep His righteous requirement, so He made provision for their sins through the blood sacrifices of animals. No one was ever "saved" by these sacrifices. These animal sacrifices were pictures of the blood atonement of the Lamb of God who would be made known in the world at a set time in history in the person of Yeshua, the Messiah.

The difference between these two covenants is this: *The covenant with Abraham was a covenant of promise based on faith. The covenant with Moses was a covenant of law based on works— His righteous requirement of His people.*

We add "covenant of law based on works" to the diagram below.

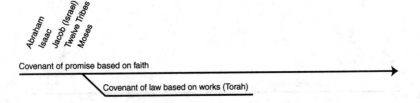

In the New Covenant days, reference to the Torah appeared to be confined to the commandments, ordinances, and statutes that were given to Moses. Much of Yeshua's and Paul's controversy with the Pharisees was over the Mosaic law and how they had turned it into a matter of works-righteousness; that is, one's righteousness was achieved through the works of the law.

Paul posed the question with the Galatians that if obedience to the law does not make us righteous, why then was it given? He answered: "It was added because of transgressions, until the Seed should come to whom the promise was made...." Gal. 3:19.

It was "added." Added to what? Added to the covenant made with Abraham! Why? Because they were not able to join Abraham in simple faith.

What an astounding thought! Had the children of Israel simply "believed" in Yahveh and in His mighty hand to deliver them, provide for them, heal them, protect them, and establish them as His royal priesthood and holy nation, there would have been no need for the law. The Torah was given because of their transgression, and their transgression was unbelief. Had they believed, as they ought, they would not have gone after other gods.

They were under the law for fifteen hundred years.

Occupying the promised land

Except for Joshua and Caleb, all who came out of Egypt died in the wilderness because they had not obeyed the voice of Yahveh. Jos. 5:6. They did not enter in because of unbelief. Joshua and Caleb survived because they had returned from spying out the land with a faith-filled report. They expressed their firm belief that Yahveh was able to make good on His promises to give them the land. The people believed the remaining spies who feared the giants in the land and brought back an evil report. Num. 14. As a result, only the second generation of Israelites who were born in the wilderness went into the land with Joshua and Caleb.

Moses was a hundred and twenty years old when he died. Deut. 34:7. Joshua succeeded him as the leader of the Israelites. Moses had laid hands on Joshua and he was full of the spirit of wisdom. The people listened to him and did what Yahveh had commanded them to do through Moses. Deut. 34:9.

The conquest

Yahveh instructed Joshua to lead the people over the Jordan to the land that He had promised to them through their forefathers. Yahveh proclaimed, "Every place that the sole of your foot shall tread upon, that have I given to you, as I said to Moses." Jos. 1:3. Yahveh read the boundaries of the deed to them once again: "From the wilderness and this Lebanon even unto the great river, the river Euphrates, all the land of the Hittites, and unto the great sea toward the going down of the sun, shall be your coast." Jos. 1:4.

Yahveh assured Joshua that no man would be able to stand before him all of the days of his life. "As I was with Moses," He said, "so will I be with you. I will not fail you, nor forsake you. Have I not commanded you? Be strong and of a good courage; be not afraid, neither be dismayed: for Yahveh your God is with you wherever you go." Jos. 1:9.

They came out of Egypt as slaves, but Yahveh used the wilderness experience to shape them into an army. They miraculously crossed over the Jordan. They supernaturally destroyed Jericho. They conquered the land as Yahveh had commanded them under the command of Joshua. The land was divided among them according to tribes except for Joseph and the Levites. The sons of Joseph, Manasseh and Ephraim, were given the inheritance of land instead of Joseph. The Levites were given cities with their common lands to live in. Jos. 21.

The promise was fulfilled. Yahveh gave them all the land that He swore to give to their fathers. They possessed it and dwelt in it. He gave them rest round about, according to all that he swore to their fathers. There stood not a man of all their enemies before them. He delivered all their enemies into their hand. He did not fail to deliver any good thing that He had spoken to them. It all came to pass. Jos. 21:43-45.

Joshua died at one hundred and ten years of age. We add Joshua to the diagram below.

Abraham Isaac Jacob (Israel) Twelve Tribes Moses Joshua

Covenant of promise based on faith

Covenant of law based on works (Torah)

Period of the Judges

Israel possessed the land, but failed to utterly drive out the enemy as Yahveh had commanded them. Consequently, they continued to war against the Philistines after Joshua's death. They did evil in the sight of Yahveh and forgot Him, plunging them time and time again into oppression. Out of their desperation, they cried out to Yahveh and repented. He raised up judges to lead them and repeatedly delivered them from their enemies.

First there was Othniel, then Ehud, Shamgar, Deborah, Gideon, Samson, and many others who were judges among them. The commentary at the end of this period sadly reads: "In those days there was no king in Israel: every man did that which was right in his own eyes." Judg. 21:25.

We add Judges to the diagram below.

Covenant of promise based on faith

Covenant of law based on works (Torah)

Saul, the first King of Israel

After the days of the judges, the word of Yahveh was rare and there was no open vision until Samuel. 1 Sam. 3:1. Samuel was born to Hannah and ministered to Yahveh with Eli in the tabernacle. He was a prophet and all Israel recognized him as a prophet and followed him.

Samuel grew old and made his two sons judges over Israel, but the sons did not walk in Samuel's way. The elders of Israel came to Samuel, demanding a king like all the other nations. This displeased Samuel. He inquired of Yahveh who answered, "Listen to the voice of the people in all that they say unto you: for they have not rejected you, but they have rejected Me, that I should not reign over them." 1 Sam. 8:7.

Yahveh wanted a people who would be a royal priesthood and a holy nation. He wanted to be king over them. He would have ruled through His prophets. But they wanted their own king. So He gave them Saul. 1 Sam. 9.

Saul was chosen by Yahveh to be king, but he did not have a heart for Yahveh nor for His will; therefore, Yahveh repented for making Saul king over Israel. 1 Sam. 15:35.

David succeeded Saul

Yahveh sent Samuel to Jesse's house to pick a king from among his sons. David was selected by Yahveh and anointed with oil by Samuel as king, but Saul was still on the throne. Saul sought several times to kill David. Eventually, Saul died in battle and David took the throne. The chronicler wrote, "So Saul died for his transgression which he committed against Yahveh, even against the word of Yahveh, which he did not keep. Also for asking counsel of one who had a familiar spirit, to inquire of her and inquired not of Yahveh: therefore He slew him, and turned the kingdom over to David the son of Jesse." 1 Chron. 10:13-14.

Davidic covenant

David had built himself a house and settled into it but did not like it that the ark of Yahveh dwelled only within curtains. He expressed to Nathan the prophet his desire to build a house for Yahveh.

Yahveh asked David a question through the prophet Nathan. "Shall you build a house for Me to dwell in?" Yahveh used this occasion to enter into covenant with David saying, "When your days are fulfilled, and you sleep with your fathers, I will set up your seed after you, which shall proceed out of your bowels, and I will establish his kingdom. He shall build a house for My name, and I will establish the throne of his kingdom forever. I will be his father, and he shall be My son. If he commits iniquity, I will chasten him with the rod of men, and with the stripes of the children of men. But My mercy shall not depart away from him, as I took it from Saul, whom I put away before you." Here is the key verse that stands as a covenant to David. *"And your [David's] house and your kingdom shall be established forever before you: your throne shall be established forever."* 2 Sam. 7:5,12-16.

A house would be built for Yahveh through David's son Solomon. David's house—that is, his royal lineage—would be established forever. Similarly, his throne would be established forever. (Also read Psalms 89.) Even though the prophetic word to build a house for Yahveh was fulfilled during Solomon's reign, the word was given to David. Solomon's throne was the same as David's throne, 2 Sam. 7:12,16, and David's throne was Yahveh's throne. 1 Chron. 29:23. David's throne and kingship pictures in the natural realm the Kingdom of Yahveh in the spiritual realm.

The apostle Paul is quoted in Acts 13:22 saying, "And when He had removed him [Saul], He raised up unto them David to be their king; to whom also He gave testimony and said, I have found David the son of Jesse, *a man after My own heart*, who shall fulfill all My will." With Saul, Yahveh gave Israel a king to satisfy their hearts. With David, He gave Himself a king to satisfy the desires of His own heart.

Israel had been given three covenants: The one made with Abraham, the one given through Moses, and this promise to David. Yet, they link together our understanding of Yahveh's eternal plan as we shall see in the unfolding of our story.

We add David to the diagram below.

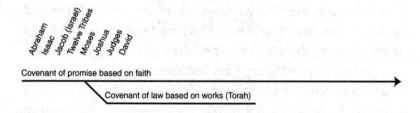

Solomon

David wanted to build the Temple as a house for Yahveh, but Yahveh did not allow him to do so because he was a man of war and had shed blood. 1 Chron. 28:3. The promise was made to David that his son Solomon would build the Temple instead. Solomon's name means peace. David had been promised that his son Solomon would be a man of rest, that he would be given rest from all his enemies round about. Peace and quiet was given to Israel during Solomon's days. 1 Chron. 22.9.

The Temple was built in 966 B.C. and the glory of Yahveh filled it. Solomon reigned as king of Israel for forty years and died.

We add Solomon to the diagram below.

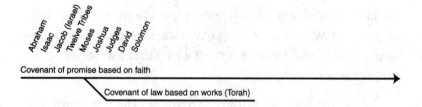

Divided Kingdom: Judah and Israel

Solomon's son, Rehoboam, was made king in his place. Rehoboam rejected the advice of the elders to lighten the burden upon the people of Israel. Consequently, Israel sent for Jeroboam and made him king. In so doing, they divided the kingdom. The kingdom of Judah to the south consisted of the tribes of Judah, Benjamin, and the Levites in their cities. The kingdom of Israel to the north consisted of the remaining tribes of Israel.

The seed of Abraham passed on through all of the tribes of Israel, but the royal seed passed through Judah, specifically through the kings of Judah as descendants of David. Rehoboam, king of Judah, was David's grandson and of the line of Judah. This was also the messianic lineage. Matt. 1:6-16. Jeroboam, King of Israel, was the son of Nebat, an Ephraimite. He had rebelled against Solomon and then Rehoboam.

We add the divided kingdom to the diagram below.

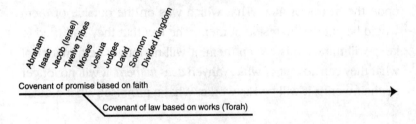

Prophets and the promise of a New Covenant

During the time of the divided kingdom Yahveh raised up many prophets. Many prophecies were given through them regarding the monarchs of the two kingdoms. The people of the northern kingdom were later referred to as Ephraim and this territory was later known as Samaria.

The prophecy that contributes significantly to our story was spoken through Jeremiah. Yahveh made a promise saying, "Behold, the days come, says Yahveh, that I will make a new covenant with the house of Israel, and with the house of Judah. Not according to the covenant that I made with their fathers in the day that I took them by the hand to bring them out of the land of Egypt which My covenant they broke, although I was a husband unto them, says Yahveh. But this shall be the covenant that I will make with the house of Israel: After those days, says Yahveh, I will put My law in their inward parts and write it in their hearts; and will be their God, and they shall be My people. They shall teach no more every man his neighbor, and every man his brother, saying, Know Yahveh: for they shall all know Me, from the least of them unto the greatest of them, says Yahveh: for I will forgive their iniquity, and I will remember their sin no more." Jer. 31:31-34 (Ezek. 11:19).

What makes this covenant new and different from the one given to Moses? The difference has to do with what it is written upon. The law that was given through Moses was written on tablets of stone. The word to Jeremiah is that the law would be written upon the hearts of men. That which was on the outside of them would be put on the inside of them. The law that they had tried to keep will miraculously keep them. It will no longer be a matter of what they can *do*, but of what Yahveh *does in them*. It will no longer be their works; it will be His works. What a promise! What a deal!

Israel/Samaria

Moses had warned the children of Israel that if they failed to observe all His commandments the curse would come upon them. Yahveh would bring a nation against them from afar, from the end of the earth, as swift as the eagle flies, a nation whose tongue they would not understand. He would scatter them among all people from one end of the earth even unto the other; and there they would serve other gods, which neither they nor their fathers knew. Deut. 28:49, 64.

Yahveh had prophesied to Moses that they would indeed be this way. He said, "Behold, you will rest with your fathers; and this people will rise and play the harlot with the gods of the foreigners of the land, where they go to be among them, and they will forsake Me and break My covenant which I have made with them." Deut. 31:16.

The harlotry of Israel and Judah is dramatically pictured in Ezekiel 23 where Yahveh portrays two sisters of harlotry. One sister is the northern kingdom of Israel (Samaria) and the other is the southern kingdom of Judah (Jerusalem). Because of this harlotry, Yahveh gave Samaria over to the Assyrians in 722 B.C. and scattered them to the nations. Thus, the ten tribes to the north were lost. Their identity as Israelites became obscure.

We add the Assyrian conquest to our diagram below.

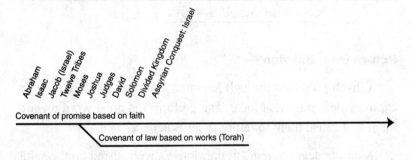

Judah

Judah saw what had happened to her older sister (Samaria) but was more corrupt than she. Judah failed to learn from her example. Thus, she was taken captive and led away into Babylon beginning in 587 B.C. Unlike her elder sister, however, Judah maintained her identity and her people were called "Jews." The term Jew derives from Judah. It primarily has to do with those who were in the southern kingdom of Judah (the tribes of Judah and Benjamin). Technically then, all Jews are Israelites, but not all Israelites are Jews.[4]

Through Jeremiah, Yahveh instructed Judah to build houses and dwell in them while in Babylon. They were to plant gardens and eat their fruit, take wives and have sons and daughters, and

---

[4] Historically, Jews were considered to be a population of people who existed in the Holy Land from the 6th century B.C. to the 1st century A.D. Religiously, Jews are descendants of the ancient Jewish people who practice one form of Judaism or another, including persons who have converted to Judaism. Ethnically, Jews are the descendants of the tribes of Judah and Benjamin.

seek the peace of the city where He had caused each of them to be carried away captive. Jer. 29:4-7.

We add the Babylonian captivity to the diagram below.

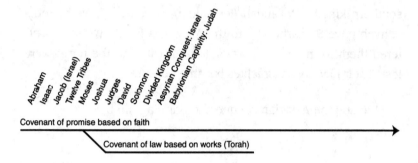

Covenant of promise based on faith

Covenant of law based on works (Torah)

Return from Babylon

Yahveh promised through Jeremiah that after seventy years in captivity He would visit Judah and perform His good word toward them and cause them to return to Jerusalem. Jer. 29:10.

After the seventy years in Babylon, Yahveh stirred up the spirit of Cyrus king of Persia to decree the return of the Jews to Jerusalem in Judah. He instructed them to build the house of Yahveh. He told them to take silver and gold, goods and livestock with them. Ezra 1.

Zerubbabel, the grandson of King Jehoiachin of Judah led the first group of Jews who returned. They rebuilt the temple between 520-516 B.C. Ezra 3:8-13.

Ezra, a scribe of the Torah, was allowed to return from exile in 458 B.C. He had prepared his heart to seek the Torah of Yahveh and to teach the statutes and judgments. Ezra. 7:6-10.

Nehemiah was the son of Hachaliah. He had been the cupbearer for king Artaxerxes in Babylon. Upon his return in 444 B.C., he governed Judah and oversaw the rebuilding of the wall around Jerusalem.

We add the return from Babylon to the diagram below.

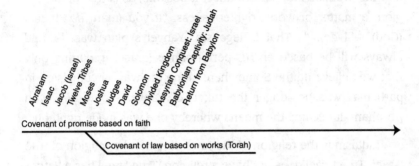

Covenant of promise based on faith

Covenant of law based on works (Torah)

Judaism

When the exiles returned from Babylon, they brought back something they had not taken with them. They brought back the embryo of a religion known today as Judaism. While some say that Judaism, as a religion, had its beginnings in Abraham and Moses, others say it began in Babylon. It is difficult to document when it really began.

We do know that the formation of the synagogues with rabbis did not exist before the Babylonian exile. By the time Yeshua came, several religious sects existed: Pharisees, Sadducees, Zealots, and Essenes. The scribes and lawyers were also woven into the fabric of religion. The code for religious behavior was very strict. The Pharisees had developed hundreds of external rules for daily living as "fence laws" to keep them a safe distance from violating the Torah. The possibility of ever keeping the whole law was out of reach.

The Jews preserved the Torah and that was good, but they did so in the context of religion. The Mosaic covenant, though they were to faithfully keep it and observe all that Yahveh had said for them to do, was in reality a picture of what Yahveh Himself promised to do. Heb. 10:1. He was their righteousness, their peace, their protector, their provider, their health and healing, and their fortress. He was their salvation.

The Jews through Judaism turned the covenant into contract and the promise into performance. It became, as is true of all religion, a matter of works-righteousness. "If you (man) *do*...then I (God) will *do*...." That is legalism. Yahveh's plan was, is, and always will be based on *His* performance (grace), requiring only that we believe (faith). Somewhere along the way, circumcision in particular was no longer the token of Yahveh's covenant with Abraham. It became the means whereby one was made righteous.

Judaism is the religion of the Jews. It is not the religion of true Israel. True Israel does not have a religion. True Israel has a Father as God. Yahveh wanted a people to be in relationship with Him through faith. He never meant for them to take those statutes and judgments (Torah) and make them the means whereby they became acceptable to Him. They were already chosen long before He gave them the Torah. Our obedience to Yahveh does not win us His favor. On the contrary, His favor toward us wins our desire to obey Him.

We draw a new line on the timeless line indicating Judaism.

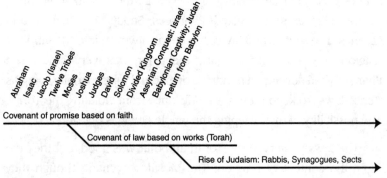

Maccabees

Between the time Yahveh spoke through Malachi, the last prophet of the Old Covenant, and the time of Yeshua's birth, 400 years passed. Several foreign powers dominated the land during these centuries: the Assyrians, the Greeks under Alexander, the kingdom of Ptolemy, and the Seleucians. The Syrian Seleucians ruled until the Jewish family of Maccabees gained independence in 143 B.C. The Jews maintained their independence until the Romans occupied the land in 63 B.C. under general Pompey.[5]

The patriarchs of Israel knew this strategic piece of land as Canaan because the Canaanites inhabited it. Abraham's descendants thought of the country as the Promised Land. The land was called Israel or the Land of Israel from the time following Joshua's conquest onward. Herodotus, the Greek "Father of History," in the 5th century B.C., was the first to call it Palestine, including part of Syria, a name that stemmed from the Philistines who were Israel's arch enemy in the land. Harper's Bible Commentary rightly affirms, "Palestine, regardless of its physical boundaries, has always been thought of as the homeland of Israelites and Jews."[6]

We add the Maccabees to the diagram below.

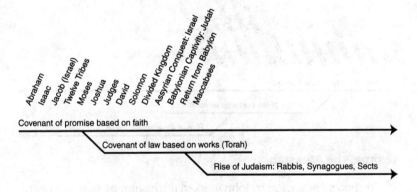

One crying in the wilderness

Then, as if the morning sun had risen on a long, dreary, and silent night, one came among them dressed in camel's hair, eating locusts and wild honey, and crying in the wilderness, "Repent, for

[5] *Nelson's Complete Book of Bible Maps & Charts—Revised and Updated Edition*, (Nashville: Thomas Nelson, 1996), p. 287.
[6] Madeleine S. Miller and J. Lane Miller, *Harper's Bible Dictionary*, 4th ed. (New York: Harper & Brothers, 1956), s.v. "Palestine."

the kingdom of heaven is at hand." His name was John. He was the first prophet through whom Yahveh had spoken to His people for four hundred years. Isaiah spoke of John saying, "The voice of one crying in the wilderness, Prepare ye the way of the Lord, make His paths straight." They came out to him from Jerusalem, Judaea, and all around the Jordan to be immersed by him in the Jordan River, confessing their sins. Matt. 3:1-6.

One day, from among the crowd a man walked forward to be immersed by John. His name was Yeshua' (Jesus) which according to Strong's Concordance means, "Jehovah [Yahveh] is salvation." John said to Him, "I need to be immersed by You. Why do you come to me?" Yeshua answered, "Allow it to be so now. It is necessary to fulfill all righteousness." So John immersed him.

We add John the Immerser to the diagram below.

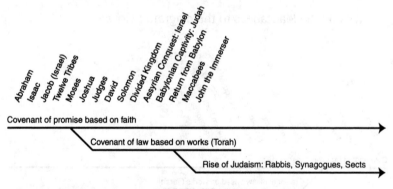

Yeshua, the Messiah

Yeshua's immersion by John marked the beginning of His ministry. His baptism was a prophetic event pointing to His eventual death, burial, and resurrection. The sequence of events that happened to Yeshua after His immersion by John directed His path to the cross where He, as the Lamb of God, would be sacrificed for the sins of the world.

---

[7] See appendix regarding the name Jesus/Yeshua.

Yeshua emerged from the Jordan and the Holy Spirit descended upon Him in the form of a dove, and God the Father spoke from heaven affirming, "This is My beloved Son in whom I am well pleased." Matt. 3:16-17.

Yeshua then passed through the crowd of on-lookers. Little did they know that this stranger from Galilee was the hope of Israel, that He had come in the fullness of time to fulfill all righteousness. All that had been veiled in Old Covenant types and shadows was being revealed to those who had eyes to see and ears to hear. He was the reality of all that had been foreshadowed. He was Yahveh's provision to make good on His promises to Abraham.

We add Yeshua and a cross through the timeless line to represent Yeshua, the Messiah.

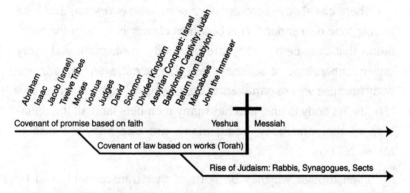

The promised seed of Abraham

Yeshua was the promised seed of Abraham. He was the transcendent seed made flesh. As Paul explained to the Galatians: "Now to Abraham and his seed were the promises made. He did not say, 'and to seeds,' as of many; but as of one, 'And to your seed,' which is Messiah." Gal. 3:16.

The mystery of the seed of Abraham is solved. Yahveh promised Abraham that through his seed he would be the father of many nations, and that all the nations of the earth would be blessed. Yeshua is that seed. Therefore, it is through Yeshua that all the nations will be blessed through faith in Him. Thus, we see clearly now what is meant by the transcendent seed.

Yeshua is from above, born of the Father; thus, He is the transcendent seed. All who are born from above by the Holy Spirit through faith are of that transcendent seed because we are in Him and He is in us. Consider a single acorn. When we look at it in the palm of our hand, it stands alone; yet, within it are all the acorns in the line that came before it and all those that will come from it. In that respect, we could say that while there were many acorns, there really is only one. Though all of the descendants of Abraham who believed were of that transcendent seed, it was always singular.

There has always been only one seed, who is Yeshua; thus, one people, one descendant. This becomes clearer in view of the revelation that "we, being many, are one body in Messiah, and every one members one of another." Rom. 12:5. We are one bread, one body because we are partakers of the one bread Messiah. 1 Cor. 10:17. "For as the body is one, and has many members, and all the members of that one body, being many, are one body: so also is Messiah." 1 Cor. 12:12.

Even though we may be born of that transcendent seed by faith, there remains only one seed and that seed brings forth the life of the "one new man" in Him. Eph. 2:15. We are all one in Him. "There is neither Jew nor Greek, there is neither bond nor free, there is neither male nor female: for you are all one in Messiah Yeshua." Gal. 3:28. There is only one body and He is the head of it. Col. 1:18. There cannot be many seeds and different bodies. There are no denominations of people in Him. Everyone whose spirit has been impregnated with the transcendent seed of Abraham, who is Yeshua, is born of Yeshua and has His life in Him. John 3:1-8.

Implanted by faith

The seed is Yeshua who was promised to Abraham and then to Isaac, Jacob, the twelve tribes, and their descendants after them. Yet, many of them did not enter into the promises of the covenant. So, how could they be of the transcendent seed and not enter in? Because the seed had to be mixed with faith! The writer of Hebrews explains, "For unto us was the gospel preached, as well as unto them [Israelites]: but the word preached did not profit them, not being mixed with faith in them that heard it." Heb. 4:2.

The seed (sperm, word) of Yahveh given to Abraham was in reality the word of Yahveh. The word of Yahveh was, is, and ever shall be Yeshua. He was the word made flesh and dwelt among us. John 1:14. When Yeshua is preached, the word (seed, sperm) of Yahveh goes out under the anointing of the Holy Spirit to bring forth revelation to men and to reproduce the Life of Yahveh.

Imperishable (incorruptible) seed

Yeshua, the transcendent seed, is also the imperishable, incorruptible seed. Peter wrote that we are born again "not of corruptible seed, but of incorruptible, by the word of God that lives and abides forever." 1 Pet. 1:23.

Abraham's natural seed (sperm) was perishable. The transcendent, covenant seed is imperishable, incorruptible. Yeshua has always been that incorruptible seed. Though He was of the line of Judah and the rightful heir to the throne of David, His father was El Elyon (God Most High). He was born of a virgin. Moreover, He never married and had no biological children of His own. Yet, all who believe in Him are born of Him with the same kind of birth as His.

Just as Yeshua was conceived by the Holy Spirit and born of the virgin Mary, so must we be born again by the Holy Spirit. We become a different kind of creature. The outward, flawed man of the flesh must perish because it is of perishable seed, but the new man of the Spirit within us is imperishable. On that glorious day of Messiah's return we will, in the twinkling of an eye, at the last trump, be raised incorruptible and be changed. "For this corruptible must put on incorruption, and this mortal must put on immortality. So when this corruptible shall have put on incorruption, and this mortal shall have put on immortality, then shall be brought to pass the saying that is written, Death is swallowed up in victory." 1 Cor. 15:52-54. When we are born of that transcendent, incorruptible seed, we become Messiah's own possession. 1 Cor. 6:20; 7:23.

Now that we are born again of that transcendent Seed and made to be like Him, we have become a transcendent people; that is to say, we have been raised up together and made to sit together in heavenly places in Messiah Yeshua. Eph. 2:6. We are going from glory to glory and from faith to faith. The more He is revealed to us the more we are becoming as He is. Transformed. Transcendent. No longer from below, but have been born from above.

Transcendent land

If we are Messiah's, then we are Abraham's seed, and heirs according to the promise. Gal. 3:29.

Seed has to have soil in which to fall, die, germinate, and reproduce. Soil is land. Abraham was promised a seed and given a land. The seed of Abraham and the land of promise belong to one another. It will never be otherwise.

As the seed is both natural and spiritual, so it is with the land. The promises pertaining to the land are to be fulfilled in the natural. The deed to the land was recorded some 4,000 years ago. No matter how many political powers have tried to possess it, nothing ever changed. The land belongs to the true Israel of Yahveh—all of it!

Yet, the natural land, as it is with Abraham's natural, biological seed, is perishable. There is a land, however, that transcends the natural and is imperishable and spiritual. Abraham was promised an earthly piece of real estate; yet, Hebrews 11:10 says that He [Abraham] looked for a city which has foundations, whose builder and maker is God." This is a city that transcends the natural.

Spiritually speaking, the souls of believers in Yeshua are this transcendent land. His seed is implanted within us with the intent of it bringing forth the promises of Abraham to us, in us, and through us.

Yeshua gave many parables associated with agriculture. Matthew records one of those. He compared people to different kinds of ground. He is the Seed and we are the ground.

We are either good or bad ground. He spoke of four types of ground in this parable: wayside, stony, thorny, and good ground. Good ground are those who hear the word and understand it, and bear fruit some a hundred-fold, some sixty, and some thirty. Matt. 13:1-23. This good ground is a land that transcends the natural and is spiritual in nature.

The will and testament of Yahveh

The land was given to Abraham and to his seed after him as an inheritance. An inheritance suggests that someone has died and left an estate to one or more benefactors. Heb. 9:16-17. There are two parties involved in this transaction: the testator who made the will and died, and the beneficiaries of the estate or inheritance.

In Yahveh's will and testament, Yahveh is the testator—the one who died through the agency of His Son. He left an inheritance. The inheritance is what He promised to Abraham.

Many unbelievers stumble over the idea that God would kill His Son or allow Him to be killed. As grievous as the death of Yeshua was, it was absolutely necessary that He die. Yeshua died in our place for our sins that we might be made righteous and thereby eligible to receive the inheritance. Being God, Yeshua's death on the cross guaranteed the promised inheritance that Yahveh covenanted with Abraham; namely, that He would be our God and we would be His people, chosen, separated, and transcendent to the praise of His glory.

In the same way that Yeshua has always been the Lamb of God, so has Yahveh's will and testament always been. It was in the heart of Father before the foundation of the earth, before any of the potential heirs were created or born.

We claim possession of our inheritance through faith in Yeshua, the Messiah. If the lawyer calls you into his office, tells you that your rich uncle just died and left you an inheritance, you can say, "I don't believe it," walk out, and miss out on your inheritance. Or you can believe it and accept it. Yahveh's will is that simple. The full deposit has been made on our behalf. We draw on it by faith. "For by grace through faith are we saved..." Eph. 2:8. He does the *grace* part; we do the *faith* part. Yet, the argument can be made that even faith is a gift from Yahveh. "Faith comes by hearing, and hearing by the *word* of Yahveh." Rom. 10:17. The Greek word for "word" in this verse is *rhema*. It is a living, spoken word which comes alive in us by revelation. It could read, "and hearing by the revelation of Yahveh." Remember how Peter came to know that Yeshua was the Messiah, the Son of the living God? Matt. 16:16-18. The Father revealed it to him.

We cannot change the will. We cannot change any of the terms of the will. We cannot determine who the heirs are. We cannot contest it. We cannot nullify it. Yahveh is the sovereign authority in all the universe. He has the final say in the matter. We who put our trust in Messiah as our Savior are "the children of Yahveh, and if children, then heirs — heirs of Yahveh, and joint-heirs with Messiah; if indeed we suffer with Him, that we may also be glorified together." Rom. 8:17 NKJV.

The blood covenant that Yahveh cut with Abraham foreshadowed Yeshua as the Lamb of Yahveh. Yahveh made the promise and sealed it with blood. Abraham believed and it was counted to him for righteousness.

Yeshua shed His blood on the cross to atone for our sins. We believe and it is counted to us for righteousness. "For the promise, that he should be the heir of the world, was not to Abraham, or to his seed, through the law, but through the righteousness of faith." Rom. 4:13. "Therefore it is of faith, that it might be by grace; to the end the promise might be sure to all the seed; not to that only which is of the law, but to that also which is of the faith of Abraham; who is the father of us all." Rom. 4:16.

Yeshua in the Old Covenant

The Old Covenant scripture from Genesis to Malachi points to Yeshua. He is the Tree of Life in the garden. Isaac, the son of promise to Abraham, was a type and shadow of Yeshua who is the Son of promise of Father-God. Yeshua is the great I AM as revealed to Moses. Ex. 3:14. Yeshua is the one of whom David spoke saying, "Yahveh said unto My Lord, Sit thou at My right hand, until I make Your enemies Your footstool." Ps. 110:1. He is the Messiah as prophesied by Isaiah. Isaiah 61:1-3; Luke 4:18-19. The Son was in the Father and the Father was in the Son. They two are one. John 17:21. He was concealed in the Old Covenant and revealed in the New.

Substitute for the Lamb

Just as the ram was a substitute for Isaac, so is Yeshua as the Lamb of God a substitute for us all. He died in our place because of our sins. In this twist of events, Isaac portrayed a likeness of us all. At first he was the lamb, but once the ram was provided, he became a type of us all who believe.

Isaac was always a son. So it is with us. When Yeshua died as the Lamb of God for us, through faith in Him, we become sons with Him. It is a mystery. We have the words for it, but the Holy Spirit has to give us understanding.

The writer of Hebrews confirms that "by faith Abraham, when he was tried [tested], offered up Isaac, and he who had received the promises was offering up his only begotten son, of whom it was said, 'That in Isaac shall your descendants [seed] be called.'" Abraham believed "that God was able to raise him even from the dead, from which he also received him back as a figure [type]." Heb. 11:17-19.

A Bride for Messiah

Isaac is also pictured as a type of Messiah who takes a bride unto Himself. Rebekah, being Isaac's wife, is a picture of the Bride of Messiah. She was the one who received the seed that brought forth the covenant offspring, Israel.

The Bride of Messiah is like Rebekah in that she is the only one who can receive the seed (word) of Yeshua and reproduce the Life of Yahveh. In order to receive the seed as the Bride, she has to be joined as one to the Bridegroom. This, too, is a mystery. One plus one equals one. We are one with Him in spirit. This union brings forth life—God's life. The husband implants the seed; the Bride bears the child. The male child of Revelation 12:1-11 is coming forth from the Bride of Messiah as manifested (revealed) sons of Yahveh who will fully and completely bear the image of their Father. Do not attempt to think of this in time because it is timeless, heavenly, and transcendent.

The Bride takes on her husband's name and finds her identity in Him. She is no longer who she used to be (a person of the flesh), but is now a new creation in Him (a person of the spirit). Consequently, her source of life is found from being one with Him by being one in Him. She is no longer her old nature, nor is she now two natures in one. She is one new nature in Him. With this change of nature comes a change of name. She is now a people who are called by His name. Acts 15:14.

Messiah means "anointed one." Yeshua is Messiah, or the Anointed One. The Bride of Messiah likewise is anointed. As He is the Messiah, then we, the Bride, are Messianics. The Greek way of expressing this is "Christ" and "Christians." The members of the Bride of Messiah are the anointed ones who are filled with the Holy Spirit and impregnated with the Word. The word is within her, transforming her into the image of the Bridegroom. "But we all, with unveiled face, beholding as in a mirror the glory of the Lord, are being transformed into the same image from glory to glory, just as from the Lord, the Spirit." 2 Cor. 3:18. "Beloved, we are now the sons of God, and it does not yet appear what we shall be but we know that, when He shall appear, we shall be like Him; for we shall see Him as He is." 1 John 3:2.

Yeshua fulfilled the covenant of Moses

Yeshua is also portrayed throughout the covenant that was made with Moses. He is pictured in the Law, the Tabernacle of Moses, the feasts, and the Sabbaths. They all speak of Him and point to Him in one way or another. Yeshua said to the Jews, "Search the scriptures; for in them you think you have eternal life: and they are *they that testify of Me.*" John 5:39.

He also said of Himself, "These are the words which I spoke unto you, while I was yet with you, that all things must be fulfilled, which were written in the law of Moses, and in the prophets, and in the psalms concerning Me." Luke 24:44.

The defining sacrificial act of Yahveh in Yeshua, the Lamb of Yahveh, brought an end to the sacrificial system that was added because of transgression. Gal. 3:19. It is no longer something we must do, because He did it for us in His life once and for all.

Previously, animal sacrifices were substitutes for the Lamb until such time as the Lamb Himself was offered up. At that time He became the Lamb once and for all as a substitute for us all—the little lambs of Yahveh. The animal sacrifices of the Old Covenant were mere shadows of the Lamb who was to come. Now that the Lamb has been revealed and offered up, it would be an abomination to the Father to offer up the substitute again. In every way, the Lamb has satisfied the Father. Faith says, Amen. If Father is satisfied with the Lamb, why would we not be satisfied? Heb. 9:11-14; 10:4.

Yeshua put an end to the shadow. For those who are reluctant to give up the shadow, my friend Bob Hughey likes to hold up a dollar bill against the light, casting its shadow against the wall. Then he asks his audience, "What would you rather have, the shadow or this dollar bill?"

Yeshua made clear that He did not come to destroy the law or the prophets, but to fulfill them. Matt. 5:17.

Yeshua met the righteous requirement of Yahveh for His people so that Yahveh might have what He promised to Abraham all along—a holy and righteous people for Himself.

We note the end of the Mosaic covenant at the foot of the cross on the timeless line diagram below.

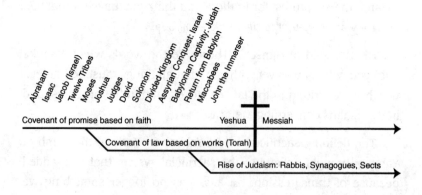

48

From the outside to the inside

As was promised, the Torah took up new residency. Where once the Torah was on the outside of Yahveh's people, written on tablets of stone as something they had to keep, now it resides within them as a power that keeps them. It is the inward power and presence of Yeshua's life. This is grace! Grace is the power of Yahveh within us that gives us the ability to *be* who we are in Yeshua and to *do* what He has made us to do.

Grace poured out the love of God upon us, so that all of the commandments of old are summed up into one new commandment—love. It has two parts: love Yahveh and love our neighbors as ourselves. Matt. 22:34-39 (Rom. 13:10; Gal. 5:14). James calls this the royal law of love. Jas. 2:8.

We do not *have* to be commanded to proclaim His name any longer because now there is within our spirit man the desire to proclaim His name. His name is wonderful and has been written on our hearts. We love His name. We are the people who are called by His name.

We do not *have* to obey the Ten Commandments any longer because now there is within our spirit man the desire to obey them. They have been written on our hearts and we love His commandments.

We do not *have* to observe the feasts any longer because they have been and are being fulfilled within us. Passover was fulfilled in us when we were born again. Pentecost was fulfilled in us when we were immersed in His Holy Spirit. Tabernacles will be fulfilled in us when we are glorified at His coming. To be glorified at His coming is to be as He is in His fullness.

The Old Covenant feasts pointed to Yeshua and He fulfilled what they were meant to picture. They were given *forever*. So in that sense they did not come to an end. They exist in Him as rep-

49

resentations of who He is and what He did to finish Father's works of redemption. They are celebrated perpetually in Messiah. The only way we can spiritually observe and celebrate the feasts in a manner that satisfies Father is to be in Messiah.

These things have been written on our hearts and He is the one who perfectly lives the fullness of them in us, because it is no longer we who live, but Messiah who lives in us. Gal. 2:20.

These observances are matters that pertain to the Kingdom of Yahveh; matters that are finished, settled, brought to rest, and established once and for all within our spirits. He is in us and we are in Him.

Compare this to a loaf of bread. As long as the loaf is on the outside of us we can see it, touch it, and smell it. But once we eat it, it becomes a part of what we are and as "they" say, we are what we eat. We can no longer see it in the natural. It enters our bodies and feeds us.

The Torah is like natural bread. It has to be "prepared and eaten" over and over again. Yeshua is the spiritual bread from heaven that keeps on living and providing life within us. When we partake of Him we partake of the feasts of Yahveh. We eat His flesh and drink His blood. The Life that is in the bread is now within us. We can look at the Bread while He is still on the outside of us and know that He has Life within for us. But that Life has no power to produce Life in us until we eat (receive) Him. We consume Him and become as He is. We have His Life more abundantly.

Grace through faith

From the beginning, in Abraham, Yahveh made a covenant of promise based on faith. Now, through the finished work of Yeshua, we are under the covenant of grace based on faith.

50

Yeshua, therefore, by His life, death, resurrection and ascension made good on Yahveh's promise to Abraham. Grace is the power within the promise to deliver the promises to all who believe. There is, therefore, a direct link between the covenant of *promise based on faith* and the covenant of *grace based on faith*. Grace is the delivery system of the promise. Grace is the extension on the timeless line of the promise.

We add, "grace through faith" to the timeless line on the diagram below.

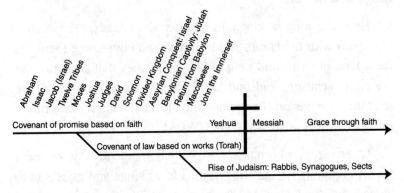

Yeshua fulfilled the Davidic covenant

Yeshua fulfilled the covenant that was made with David that his throne would be forever. The Seed (Yeshua) is of the Davidic lineage. He is the King who sits on David's throne. The angel spoke prophetically to Mary regarding her conception of Yeshua saying, "You shall conceive in your womb, and bring forth a son and shall call His name Yeshua. He shall be great, and shall be called the Son of the Highest: and the Lord God shall give unto Him the throne of his father David: And he shall reign over the house of Jacob forever; and of His kingdom there shall be no end." Luke 1:30-33.

Yahveh said to Solomon, "Then will I establish the throne of your kingdom, according as I have covenanted with David your

father, saying, You shall not fail to have a man to be ruler in Israel."
2 Chron. 7:18. Yeshua is the final king to sit on David's throne. No
other king is needed to follow Him. Though He does not appear to
be sitting on the throne in the natural realm, He is very much there
in the heavenlies. His kingdom is not of this world. John 18:36. It is
within us who believe in Yeshua. David's throne is established forever in Yeshua.

Kings and priests

He is the King of kings. Revelation 17:14 reads, "These shall
make war with the Lamb, and the Lamb shall overcome them: for
He is Lord of lords, and King of kings: and they that are with Him
are called, chosen, and faithful." Again, in Revelation 19:16, we
read that "He has on His vesture and on His thigh a name written,
KING OF KINGS, AND LORD OF LORDS."

When we were born again, we were born into royalty. We learn
from Revelation 1:6 that He "has made us kings and priests unto
Yahveh and His Father; to Him be glory and dominion forever and
ever." And in Revelation 5:10 we see that He has "made us unto our
God kings and priests: and we shall reign on the earth." He is the
King and we are kings. We rule with Him as kings. As He said to
Jacob when He changed his name to Israel, of whom we are, "for as
a prince you have power with God and with men..." Gen. 32:28.

Additionally, Yeshua not only is King, but is also a priest according to the order of the Melchizedek priesthood. Melchizedek means,
"king of righteousness." He was the king of Salem (peace) and priest
of El Elyon (God Most High) to whom Abram paid a tithe after Lot
was rescued. Gen. 14 and Heb. 7. David prophesied regarding the coming Messiah, "Yahveh has sworn, and will not repent, You are a
priest forever after the order of Melchizedek." Ps. 110:4. Melchizedek

was both king and priest. He came bringing bread and wine, representing the blood atonement of Messiah yet to be revealed.

Seed produces according to its own kind. If we are born of His transcendent and imperishable seed, then we have His transcendent and imperishable nature. Moreover, we who are the people of this transcendent and imperishable seed are of the Melchizedek order of priesthood just as was Messiah. Therefore, we who are in Him are kings and priests.

In Yeshua, Yahveh now has the desire of His heart as expressed through Moses—a kingdom of priests and an holy nation. Exod. 19:6. Peter confirms that we who believe in Yeshua are "a chosen generation, a royal priesthood, an holy nation, a peculiar people that you [we] should show forth the praises of Him who has called us out of darkness into His marvelous light." 1 Pet. 2:9.

True Jews

Moreover, those who put their trust in Yeshua are the true Jews. Paul wrote, "For he is not a Jew who is one outwardly; neither is that circumcision, which is outward in the flesh. But he is a Jew who is one inwardly; and circumcision is that of the heart, in the spirit, and not in the letter; whose praise is not of men, but of Yahveh." Rom. 2:28-29.

If we are born of Yeshua who is of the line of Judah, then we are of the line of Judah. Thus, we are the true Jews, heirs and joint-heirs with Messiah of the promises of Abraham. He is the one who then circumcises our hearts.

There is no difference between those of us who are in Yeshua. We are one in Him "where there is neither Greek nor Jew, circumcision nor uncircumcision, Barbarian, Scythian, bond nor free: but Messiah is all, and in all." Col. 3:11.

Satisfied!

Yahveh knew from the beginning that His people would not be able to fulfill the righteous requirement of the Torah. He knew that He and He alone could fulfill it, because He is The Righteous One. He is our righteousness. There is no good thing in us that would make us capable of satisfying Father's righteous requirement.

The sacrificial Lamb has always been in the Father. Yeshua, Messiah, as the Lamb of Yahveh, was not an after-thought. He was not Plan B. He always was, and ever shall be.

As Yeshua breathed His last upon the cross, He cried, "It is finished." Father looked down from heaven and was satisfied. Yeshua did for us what we could not do for ourselves. *He satisfied the Father's righteous requirement set forth by the Torah.* Additionally, He took our sins upon Himself enabling us to be acceptable to the Father. Yeshua finished the work of Yahveh. Yeshua is the finished work of Yahveh. Nothing can be added to or taken away from His work. Yeshua *plus* anything leads to legalistic bondage and death. It is heresy.

In Abraham, Yahveh entered into a covenant of promise based on faith. In so doing, He formed a people for Himself.

Through Moses, Yahveh entered into a covenant of law based on works. In so doing, He set forth the righteous requirement for His people.

Now in Yeshua, through His shed blood, Yahveh purchased the people He formed in Abraham. In so doing, He entered into a new covenant of grace based on faith, making good on His promise to Abraham.

We add "'satisfied" above the cross on the timeless line below.

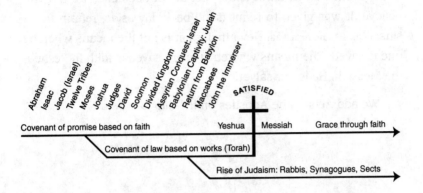

Circumcision party

The period of time immediately following Yeshua's ascension is commonly referred to in scripture as the Acts of the Apostles. True believers clearly understood the wonder-working, liberating power of His grace that had set them free from the bondage of the law. However, some of those who professed to believe in Messiah did not understand the power of Yahveh's grace. They did not appreciate the liberty that Yeshua had purchased for them. They wanted the Gentile believers to be circumcised as Jews before they could be accepted as true believers in Messiah.

These people were called the circumcision party or Judaizers. They did not understand that what was once on the outside of them to govern them, now governed them from within. They did not understand that circumcision was no longer a matter of the flesh, but of the heart.

The outward sign of that inward circumcision is water baptism (immersion).[8] Water baptism is not the means whereby we are saved, but it is the *sign* that we have confessed with our mouths and believed in our hearts that Yeshua is Lord. Water baptism is

---

[8] The Greek word for baptism means to dip or immerse. Different Greek words exist for sprinkling and pouring.

very important. It is essential that everyone be immersed in water in the name of Yeshua. It is the first act of obedience for all who believe. It was given to remit (send back, lay aside, refrain from) sins. Mark 1:4 and Acts 2:38. Nevertheless, it is not the means whereby one is saved. The means whereby we are saved is faith in Yeshua, the Messiah. He is our salvation.

We add Acts of the Apostles on the diagram below.

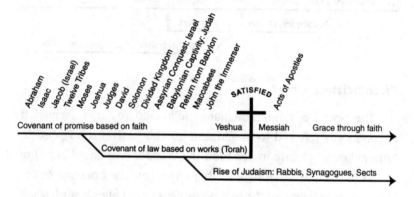

The solidification of Judaism

Jerusalem fell at the hands of the Romans in 70 A.D. at which time the temple was destroyed. The Jews no longer had a center of worship and could no longer offer up animal sacrifices. Changes were needed in how they expressed themselves religiously.

Rabbis in the first and second centuries began to commit to writing, in addition to the Torah, other ancient oral laws, customs, and rituals that governed Jewish society, resulting in what is known as the Talmud ("learning" or "study"). The Talmud was completed in the third century A.D. under the authority of Rabbi Judah ha-Nasi, head of the Jewish community in what became known as Palestine. The primary section of the Talmud is the Mishna ("repeated study") which is the code of religious and civil laws governing society. The other section of the Talmud is the Gemara ("completion") which consist of commentaries on the Mishna. There was a Palestinian and Babylonian Talmud. The Palestinian Talmud was not completed because Palestine had become largely Christian by the end of the fourth century and the academies ceased to exist. The Babylonian Talmud became the standard text of Jewish law and religion. Orthodox believers consider the Talmud as being divinely inspired. The Talmud, more than anything, defined Judaism as a religion from that time on.[9]

Early church fathers

Soon after the old apostle John died at the end of the first century A.D., not much history was recorded pertaining to the life and events of the called-out-ones. When the pages began to turn again into the second century A.D., we find men contending for positions of ecclesiastical rule over cities, and they had given themselves the title of Bishop. Without realizing the consequences of their ambition for power and position, they took on the nicolaitan spirit. Rev. 2:6,15. Nicolaitan in the Greek translates, "conqueror of the laity (people)." This was the embryo of the clergy system. The concept of church[10] as an institution with positions of authority began to take shape. A new religion had begun.

The Nicolaitans, like the religious leaders in Judaism, turned the precious covenant of grace through faith into contract, laying down laws and rules of religious behavior of their own making. Believers gradually and very subtly became subjected to the tyranny of the clergy. They fashioned a religious system around their spiritual experiences.

Christianity

The full-term birthing of this new religion took place when Constantine was Emperor of Rome. He was converted to

---

[9] *2000 Compton's Encyclopedia and Fact Index,* s.v. "Talmud."

[10] When the word *church* appears in italics it is in reference to the institutional system or to a building.

Christianity and decreed the Edict of Milan in 313 A.D. that mandated toleration of Christians in the Roman Empire. The Christian faith became Constantine's favorite religion and he became the "guardian" of the church. The church was given legal rights and large financial donations. He intervened in church affairs, presiding over the first ecumenical council of the church at Nicaea in 325 A.D. He built churches in the Holy Land. He set the stage for the entrenchment of Christianity as a religion at the end of the fourth century. He is considered a major figure in the foundation of Medieval Christian Europe.[11] Christianity as a world religion today spreads across the spectrum of Roman Catholicism, Greek Orthodoxy, all Protestant denominations, and the multitude of independent church offspring.

We add Constantine and a new line to the diagram signifying Christianity as a religion, running parallel with Judaism.

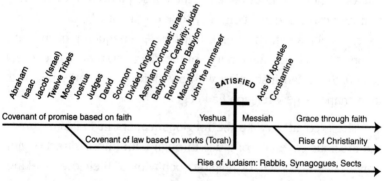

"Us and them"

With the existence of these two religions—Judaism and Christianity—we now have an "us" and "them"! There can be no "us" and "them" in Yeshua. There is and always has been only one covenant God and one covenant people beginning with Abraham unto this present day. There is only one assembly, the Israel of

---

[11] *Microsoft Encarta 96 Encyclopedia*, s.v. "Constantine the Great."

Yahveh. These two religions have little association with the Abrahamic covenant. The promises made to Abraham are not achieved by adherence to any religion. The promises were not made to a religion, but to a chosen people.

The term *church* is not only a mistranslation of the Greek word *ekklesia* (assembly of called-out-ones), but also conveys a wrong theology regarding who we are as Abraham's seed in Yeshua. We tend to think along the lines that on the one hand there are the Jews and on the other hand there is the *church*. Some people even hold to the erroneous "replacement" theology that claims that the church or Christianity is the only true Israel. They believe that after God judged the Israel of the Old Covenant, He gave her commission to the church of the New Covenant.

Yeshua had no thought of His *ekklesia* being something other than the continuation of His *qahal* in the Old Covenant. *Qahal* means "assembly" and is the equivalent to the Greek *ekklesia*.[12]

When Yeshua pronounced to Peter and the other disciples with Him, "Upon this rock [of revelation] I will build My *ekklesia* [assembly of called-out-ones]," He was referring to the one and only assembly of Yahveh throughout history. Israel was the *qahal* of Yahveh. The *ekklesia* is the *qahal* of Yahveh. They are one and the same. Yeshua was saying in effect that the assembly of Yahveh are those who respond in faith (faithfulness) to Yahveh through Yeshua whether looking forward to Him by faith or looking back upon Him by faith.

We really do need to repent from using the word "church" in reference to the *ekklesia*. It will always fail to communicate the truth. If we use "called-out-ones" or "assembly of called-out-ones" in place of "church" when reading the New Covenant, we

---

[12] We know this because *ekklesia* was chosen to translate the Hebrew word *qahal* from Hebrew to Greek in the Septuagint. The Septuagint is the Greek translation of the Hebrew Old Testament that was done by Jewish scholars in the third and second centuries B.C.

will see how it changes our perspective on the passage. Reading it this way enables us to get past our institutionalized, organized *church* systems grid.

Middles Ages

The Middle Ages (that period of European history from about 500 to 1500 A.D.) has been characterized as the dark ages. This designation of the times proved characteristic of Christianity as a religion as well. Roman Catholicism crystallized Christianity as a religion with the rise of the pope to power, the evolving of the hierarchy of the clergy, the establishment of abusive religious orders, the practice of indulgences, and the further amalgamation of Christian doctrine with paganism—just to name a few.

We add the Middle Ages to our diagram.

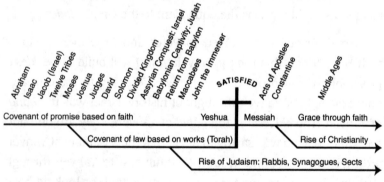

Modern Judaizers

This brings us to modern times. For two millenniums, Christian zealots (Christianizers) desired to convert the Jews from Judaism to adhere to the tenets of Christianity, asking them essentially to trade one religion for another, thinking that in so doing the Jews would be saved. Why would anyone want to swap one religion for another? Religion has never saved a soul. Thankfully, many Jews have accepted Yeshua as their Messiah and have had genuine conversion experiences. Some have become Christianized and joined *churches.* Many others have formed Messianic congregations, preserving to various degrees their heritage as Jews.

Now, we face a strange phenomenon. Many Christians are rejecting the bondage they experienced in the idolatrous *church* systems and are turning to what they call "their Hebraic roots." Many of them observe the feasts and Sabbaths sincerely desiring to please God. They reason that since Yeshua kept the feasts and Sabbaths so ought others. Certainly, Yeshua observed the feasts and the Sabbaths because He perfectly fulfilled the law. He was fulfilling for us in His natural life the righteous requirements of Yahveh for His covenant people. He was doing for us what He required of us, yet we could not do for ourselves.

Torah observant believers further justify their practice because these feasts were given perpetually, eternally. In fact they were. Yeshua said that He did not come to destroy (abolish) the law and the prophets, but to fulfill them. Matt. 5:17. He did not destroy them, but something different happened. These feasts under the Old Covenant were earthy expressions of a heavenly reality. They have always existed. They exist now and ever shall exist in the realm of the kingdom. They have always represented Yahveh's finished work in Yeshua. They express Him and He expresses them. They are perpetually celebrated in who Yeshua is and what He did. They transcend the earthly in that they are resident within the Transcendent One. We thereby celebrate them spiritually by being in Him and by Him being in us. We celebrate them when we celebrate Him. They were not done away with but are perpetually observed in heavenly places where we sit with Him.

Many Torah observant believers today have deified Christianized versions of the customs, traditions, and practices of Judaism. Others, more radical than these, have gone back under the law, requiring this of others. These are undeniably modern day Judaizers.

It does not end here. Modern day Judaizers are those who also would impose any form of religious doctrines or self-works upon us as a means of earning our salvation or coming into the good "graces" of Messiah, our Savior. Many among us preach the doctrines of men as though they were the gospel (good news). They make faith, baptism, prosperity, Sabbath observance, dietary laws, sonship, and many other themes the gospel they preach. While there may be some truth in these revelations, they are not the gospel. Yeshua and Him crucified is the good news. 1 Cor. 1:23.

Paul marveled at how quickly the Galatian believers were so removed from the grace of Messiah by the teachings of the Judaizers. They were believing another gospel, although he quickly established that it was a perversion of the gospel. With a very powerful stroke of the pen he exhorted them saying, "Though we, or an angel from heaven, preach any other gospel unto you than that which we have preached unto you, let him be accursed." Gal. 1:6-9. He meant business, repeating it a second time.

Certainly, observing the feasts outwardly may be of value as long as we clearly understand we are not doing it for the sake of gaining our righteousness. It is good for all believers to know the significance of the Old Covenant laws, feasts, tabernacle, and Sabbaths and to see how these things point to Yahveh's finished work in Yeshua. These are appropriate occasions to celebrate Yeshua. If we celebrate Passover, we celebrate the Passover Lamb, Yeshua. If we celebrate Pentecost, we celebrate Yeshua, the firstfruits and the giving of the Holy Spirit. If we celebrate Tabernacles, we celebrate Yeshua's ingathering of His people unto Himself. But these things can never be done in an "ought-to" manner.

Yahveh may truly be calling attention to the Torah and His feasts today and we want to pay attention to that. The human tendency, however, as has been true of most other past moves of God, is to put our hands on what He is doing, pervert it, and thereby kill it. If possible, we will package and merchandize it to death. We end up with something other than what He wanted. We must guard our hearts and not lose sight of the absolute, glorious liberty we have in Yeshua.

Jews do not have to convert to "Christianity" to be believers in Yeshua. They do not have to give up their Jewish identity to become believers in Yeshua as Messiah. In fact, according to this timeless line, the Jews' belief in Yeshua as Messiah positions them as true heirs of the covenant Yahveh made with Abraham. They are born of that transcendent seed.

Yahveh calls us to abandon all religion whether Judaism, Christianity, Islam, Hinduism, Buddhism, or any other. He calls us into a relationship with Him through faith in Yeshua whereby we become heirs of the promises to Abraham.

Falling from grace

The apostle Paul clearly explained the risk run by born-again believers who go back under the law. He charged the Galatians to stand fast in the liberty wherewith Messiah had made them free. He warned them not to be entangled again with the yoke of bondage, referring to the law. "If you are circumcised," he wrote, "Messiah shall profit you nothing. I testify again to every man who is circumcised, that he is a debtor to do the whole law. Messiah has become of no effect unto you. Whosoever of you are justified by the law; you are fallen from grace." Gal. 5:1-4. Please note that *falling from grace* is not falling into sin, but *is what happens to us when we go back under the law.* Moreover, the law arouses our emotions (passions) of sin. Rom. 7:5 NKJV.

We will either live free under grace or live in bondage under the law. Make the comparison and choose between the two: shadow or reality, law or grace, works or rest, outside or inside, flesh or spirit, earthly or heavenly, unbelief or faith, disobedience or obedience, death or life.

Any other so-called gospel is not the gospel, but is deceptive and deadly. Therefore, beware of the circumcision party among you and within you!

The restoration of natural Israel

The transcendent seed that was in the Northern Kingdom of Israel—those scattered to the nations—passed through the sons of their foreign wives. After several generations they had the appearances of other ethnic groups—wherever they had been scattered. They became Oriental, African, Anglo-Saxon, and so on. After several generations, they no longer knew that they were of the seed of Abraham and remembered nothing of the covenant with its promises, but Yahveh knew. Yahveh knew where every one of His seed had been scattered, and He promised to Jeremiah that He would gather the remnant of His flock out of all countries where He had driven them and would bring them again to their folds. They would dwell in their own land. Jer. 23:3-8.

Numerous restoration prophecies are spoken of in the Old and the New Covenants that we simply cannot ignore. The prophet Ezekiel was told by Yahveh to take two sticks. He was to write "Judah" on one of the sticks and "Joseph" on the other. Judah represented the Southern Kingdom of Judah. Joseph (also called Ephraim) represented the Northern Kingdom of Israel. These are also called the two houses of Israel. Ezekiel was to join the sticks together to become one in his hand. He was to explain to the people that Yahveh would be taking these two sticks (houses) and making them one in His hand. Speaking for Yahveh he said, "Look, I will take the sons of Israel from among the nations where they have gone, and I will gather them from every side and bring them into their own land. I will make them one nation in the land, on the mountains of Israel. One king will be king for all of them and they will no longer be two nations and no longer be divided into two kingdoms." Ezek. 37:15-28. This has not taken place in history

64

between natural Israel and Judah. It is yet to come. What Yahveh promises will come about. His promises to Israel are everlasting.

Israel's blindness continues until the times of the Gentiles (nations, heathens) are fulfilled. Luke 21:24. After that, the veil will be lifted from Israel's eyes and they will return to Yahveh, their God. 2 Cor. 3:13-16. Paul wrote regarding Israel's status, "What then? Israel has not obtained that which he seeks for; but the election has obtained it, and the rest were blinded (According as it is written, God has given them the spirit of slumber, eyes that they should not see, and ears that they should not hear;) unto this day. And David said, Let their table be made a snare, and a trap, and a stumbling block, and a recompense unto them: Let their eyes be darkened, that they may not see, and bow down their backs always. I say then, have they stumbled that they should fall? God forbid: but rather through their fall salvation has come unto the Gentiles, to provoke them to jealousy. Now if their fall is for the riches of the world, and their diminishing is for the riches of the Gentiles; *how much more their fullness?"* Rom. 11:7-12.

A partial restoration has already taken place. Thousands of Jews began migrating back to their homeland after the turn of the twentieth century and, against numerous odds, became a nation in 1948. Jerusalem was recaptured in 1967. The struggle between Israel and the descendants of Ishmael who call themselves Palestinians prevails to this present time. The fullness of this return is yet to come. Judah and Israel will be made one.

Judah and Israel have endured much persecution, rejection, and suffering throughout their history. The world and many within the *church* have essentially written Israel off. But let us be sure of this one thing: every act of judgment and destruction to Israel for her iniquities and idolatries by Yahveh was followed by a promise of restoration.

Natural Israel as a people in the land of Israel is Yahveh's prophetic clock, counting down His time of restoration. We see the unfolding of His story being told as prophesied of old. This restoration is a work that only Yahveh can do in His set time.

We add the restoration of the house of Judah and the house of Israel to our diagram.

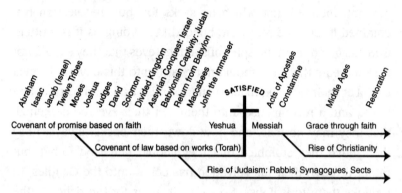

The End of the Ages

From here onward, we await the fulfillment of Tabernacles and the manifestation of the sons of Yahveh as promised in Romans 8:19, "For the earnest expectation of the creature waits for the manifestation of the sons of God."

For Yahveh's sake

Knowing that we who believe are of the transcendent seed of Abraham impacts our understanding of the gospel of the Kingdom of Yahveh. We now understand that we are a people by Him and for Him. We understand that He knew us before the foundation of the world, that He chose us, that He created us for His sake and not for our own sake.

Yet, for the most part, we have grown up under a self-sake gospel that erroneously preaches that Yahveh exists to save us so we can live abundant lives in this world, miss hell, and go to heaven when we die. The focus is upon us. Consequently, we view God as someone we have to bargain with to get what we think we want and need for our sakes. We also view Him as someone who is hard to please and all but a few will make it in.

This is a self-seeking gospel and we were not created for that. We were created by and for Yahveh that He might have a people of His own. We were not saved for our sakes, but for His sake. (When we try to live our lives for our sakes—trying to fashion our lives in contradiction to His eternal intentions—we live frustrated, empty, and defeated lives. We miss our purpose for existence.) Our lives are not the lives He wants for us to live. His life is the life He wants for us to live. Gal. 2:20. He wants to live His life *in* us and *through* us *as* us. Therefore we are to live in the faith of the Son of God in order for Him to have what He wants.

When we see our existence from Yahveh's perspective, it literally catapults us into a much higher realm of reality. We have a focused sense of purpose that produces a peace that passes all understanding. When we surrender ourselves to Him so that He can have what He wants, ironically, we are given life more abundantly. We must be apprehended by the knowledge that we are not our own, but have been bought with a price. 1 Cor. 6:19-20.

Moreover, this revelation that we exist for Him wipes out all foolish notions that we have anything to do with our salvation. Since He created us, and called and chose us for Himself, then it is totally up to Him to do what He has promised for Himself: to conform us into the image of His Son. He wants this more than we do. We should want it as much as He does.

"But we all, with open face beholding as in a glass the glory of the Lord, are changed into the same image from glory to glory, even as by the Spirit of the Lord." 2 Cor. 3:18.

"For whom He foreknew, He also predestined to be conformed to the image of His Son, that He [the Son] might be the firstborn among many brethren. Moreover whom He did predestine, them He also called: and whom He called, them He also justified: and whom He justified, them He also glorified." Rom. 8:29-30.

"For we are His workmanship, created in Messiah Yeshua unto good works, which God has before ordained that we should walk in them." Eph. 2:10.

"Being confident of this very thing, that He who began a good work in you will perform it until the day of Yeshua Messiah." Phil. 1:6.

From His perspective, we are in Messiah and He is in us; and, thereby, we are new creatures. Old things have passed away and all things have become new. 2 Cor. 5:17. Consequently, He "has raised us up together, and made us sit together in heavenly places in Messiah Yeshua." Eph. 2:6. That's all His part. Our part is to believe. "Yeshua answered and said unto them, This is the work of God, that you believe on Him whom He has sent." John 6:29. We believe in the finished work of Messiah on the cross. If Yeshua satisfied the Father, we ought also to be satisfied with Him and what He finished for the Father. If we truly believe, we will love Him; if we love Him, we will obey Him.

Conclusion

Therefore, let us cease from thinking we were created and saved for our sakes. We were created and saved for His sake. It is not about us. It is all about Him. Know *whose* you are and *who* you are in Messiah Yeshua and you will know *why* you are, *what* you are, and *where* you are—created for Him as a son of His and seated with Him in heavenly places. That revelation will utterly transform you.

We who believe in Yahveh through faith in Yeshua are of the transcendent seed of Abraham—the transcendent people for Yahveh, the people of this timeless line, a holy habitation for Yahveh in the spirit.

"For all the promises of Yahveh in Yeshua are yes, and in Him Amen, unto the glory of God by us." 2 Cor. 1:20.